**to horse around**
*to play in a rowdy way*

**monkey business**
*silly behavior*

# THERE'S A FROG IN MY THROAT!
## 440 Animal Sayings a Little Bird Told Me

written by
## Loreen Leedy & Pat Street

illustrated by
## Loreen Leedy

**lucky duck**
*fortunate person*

Holiday House
New York

**It's the cat's meow!**
*It's terrific!*

meow!

to turn turtle
*to turn upside down*

We love animal sayings! Sayings pack a lot of meaning into a few words. Plus, it's just more fun to say "It's raining cats and dogs" than "It's raining hard."

Every language has its own unique sayings. For this book, we collected 440 of our favorite animal sayings in English. As you will see, many of them compare people to animals.

A **simile** makes a comparison using the word *like* or the word *as*. If someone is "as quiet as a mouse," that person is silent. (Mice aren't noisy.)

A **metaphor** also makes a comparison, but without *like* or *as*. If someone is a "night owl," he or she likes to stay up late. (Owls are active at night.)

An **idiom** doesn't mean exactly what the words say. For example, "She has butterflies in her stomach" doesn't mean she's eaten some butterflies! Instead, it means "She feels nervous."

A **proverb** gives advice about how to act in daily life. For example, to advise someone not to exaggerate a problem, you can say, "Don't make a mountain out of a molehill."

We fit as many animal sayings into these pages as we could—even a few about feathers and shells and fur and tails. Most of these sayings are well known, but we think some will be new to you. We included one common meaning for each saying. (Some have more than one meaning.)

Happy reading! We hope you will enjoy this book "till the cows come home"—for a very long time!

**See you later, alligator!**
Loreen Leedy and Pat Street

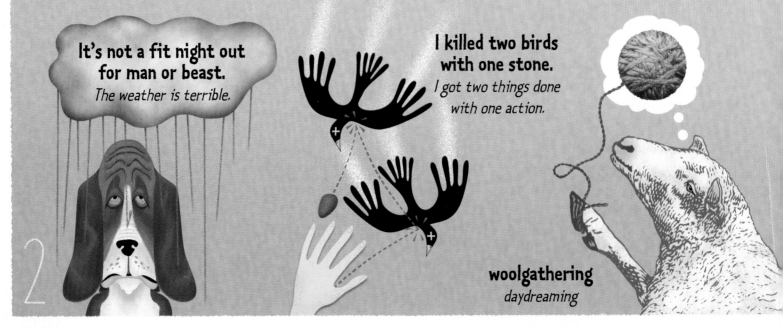

**It's not a fit night out for man or beast.**
*The weather is terrible.*

**I killed two birds with one stone.**
*I got two things done with one action.*

**woolgathering**
*daydreaming*

2

# contents

We're off like a herd of turtles.
*We're getting a slow start.*

Let's tie on the old feed bag.
*Let's eat.*

What's the buzz?
*What are people saying?*

It's the bee's knees!
*It's terrific!*

I put my head in the lion's mouth.
*I took a big risk.*

3

**This place is going to the dogs.**
*Things are getting worse and worse.*

**dog-eared page**
*folded page corner*

**Let sleeping dogs lie.**
*Leave old problems alone.*

**Stop hounding me!**
*Stop pestering me!*

**Hot dog!**
*Wow!*

**You're barking up the wrong tree.**
*You've got the wrong idea.*

**You can't teach an old dog new tricks.**
*It's harder for an older person to learn new things.*

**His bark is worse than his bite.**
*He's not as fierce as he seems.*

**It's a dog-eat-dog world.**
*Life can be brutally competitive.*

**You lie like a dog.**
*You're telling a lie.*

**putting on the dog**
*wearing fancy clothes*

**autograph hound**
*signature collector*

Mark Magrowl  Meryl Sheep  Tom Chews  Julia Rabbits

**Don't bite the hand that feeds you.**
*Don't harm someone who is helping you.*

**That dog won't hunt.**
*That idea won't work.*

**She's on the scent.**
*She is tracking it down.*

**She's dogging my footsteps.**
*She's following me.*

dogleg
*sharp bend in a path*

**I've been working like a dog.**
*I've been working very hard.*

**His tail was between his legs.**
*He was ashamed.*

**dog years**
*1 human year =* 7 *dog years*

The tail is wagging the dog. *A small part is controlling the whole thing.*

**They fight like cats and dogs.** *They have fierce arguments.*

The fur is going to fly. *There will be a big fight.*

They put on a dog-and-pony show. *They gave us a fancy sales pitch.*

to do the
doggie paddle
*to swim
like a dog*

**It's raining cats and dogs.** *It's raining hard.*

It's a three-dog night. *It's very cold.*

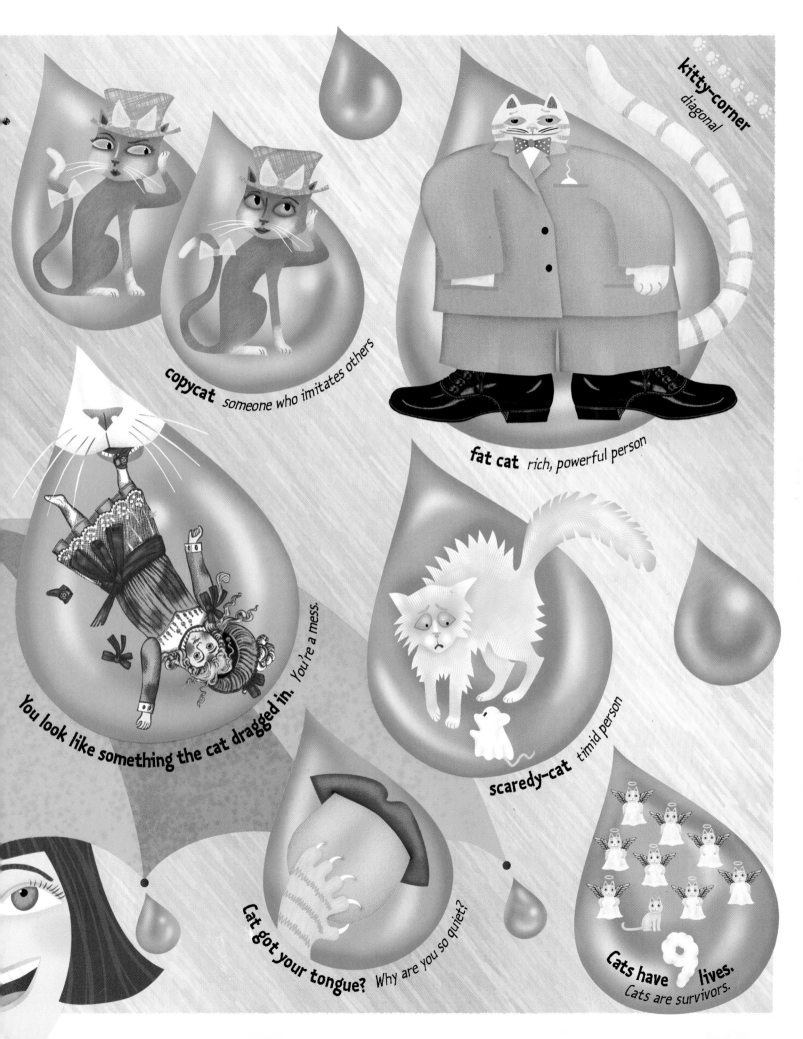

**kitty-corner** *diagonal*

**copycat** *someone who imitates others*

**fat cat** *rich, powerful person*

**You look like something the cat dragged in.** *You're a mess.*

**scaredy-cat** *timid person*

**Cat got your tongue?** *Why are you so quiet?*

**Cats have 9 lives.** *Cats are survivors.*

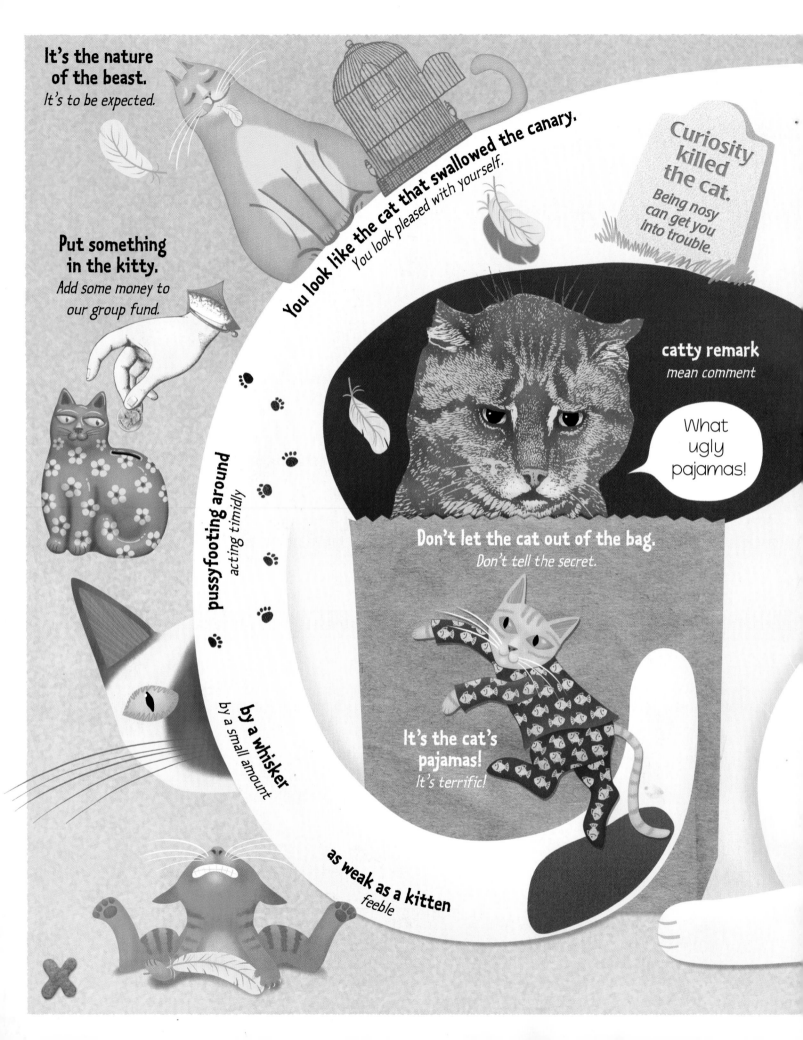

**When the cat's away, the mice will play.**
Workers goof off when the boss is gone.

**Are you a man or a mouse?**
Are you brave or cowardly?

**as quiet as a mouse**
silent

**Who will bell the cat?**
Who will face danger for the good of us all?

**to build a better mousetrap**
to invent or improve a product

**to play cat and mouse**
to cruelly toy with someone

**catnap**
short period of sleep

**mouse potato**
frequent computer user

He pulled a rabbit out of a hat. He did something amazing.

I'm the guinea pig. I'm the first to try it.

The bird has flown. The person has left.

I'm on the hamster wheel. My work seems endless.

She will ferret it out. She will look everywhere until she finds it.

She parrots his words. She mindlessly repeats what he says.

**Birdbrain!**
*You're stupid!*

**Birdbrain!**
*You're stupid!*

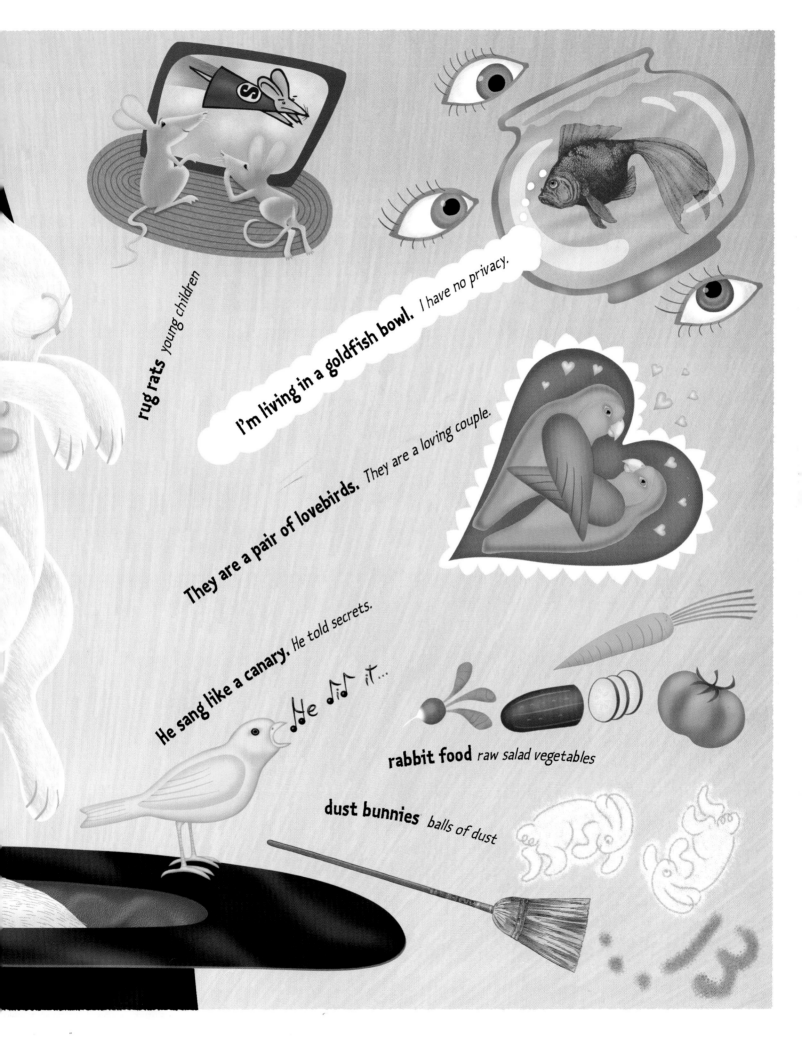

rug rats *young children*

I'm living in a goldfish bowl. *I have no privacy.*

They are a pair of lovebirds. *They are a loving couple.*

He sang like a canary. *He told secrets.*

He 🎵 it...

rabbit food *raw salad vegetables*

dust bunnies *balls of dust*

# on the FARM

**I'm walking on eggs.**
*I'm being careful not to offend someone.*

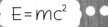
$E = mc^2$ ....

**egghead**
*highly educated person*

**Which came first, the chicken or the egg?**
*We don't know which event caused the other.*

**hen fruit**
*chicken eggs*

**You can't unscramble eggs.**
*What's done is done.*

**good egg**
*nice person*

**bad egg**
*terrible person*

**Don't put all your eggs in one basket.**
*Spread out your risk in more than one place.*

**I rule the roost!**
*I'm the boss!*

**to crow about it**
*to brag about it*

**dumb cluck**
*person who is acting stupid*

**I can only hunt and peck.**
*I'm a poor typist.*

**Does a chicken have lips?**
*No, no, no!*

**She took me under her wing.**
*She sheltered and guided me.*

**mother hen**
*protective person*

**Don't count your chickens before they hatch.**
*You can't plan on having something until you actually get it.*

**We laid an egg.**
*Our performance was awful.*

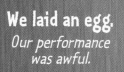

**I got egg on my face.**
*I was humiliated.*

**The chickens have come home to roost.**
*You did something wrong, and now it has caught up with you.*

15

**I don't want to hear another peep out of you!**
*Be quiet!*

Peep!

**as mad as a wet hen**
*furious*

**There's nobody here but us chickens.**
*We're the only ones here.*

**You're letting the fox guard the henhouse.**
*You're putting the wrong person in charge.*

**She gets up with the chickens.**
*She wakes up early in the morning.*

**She is first in the pecking order.**
*She has the top rank in our group.*

**chicken feed**
*small amount of money*

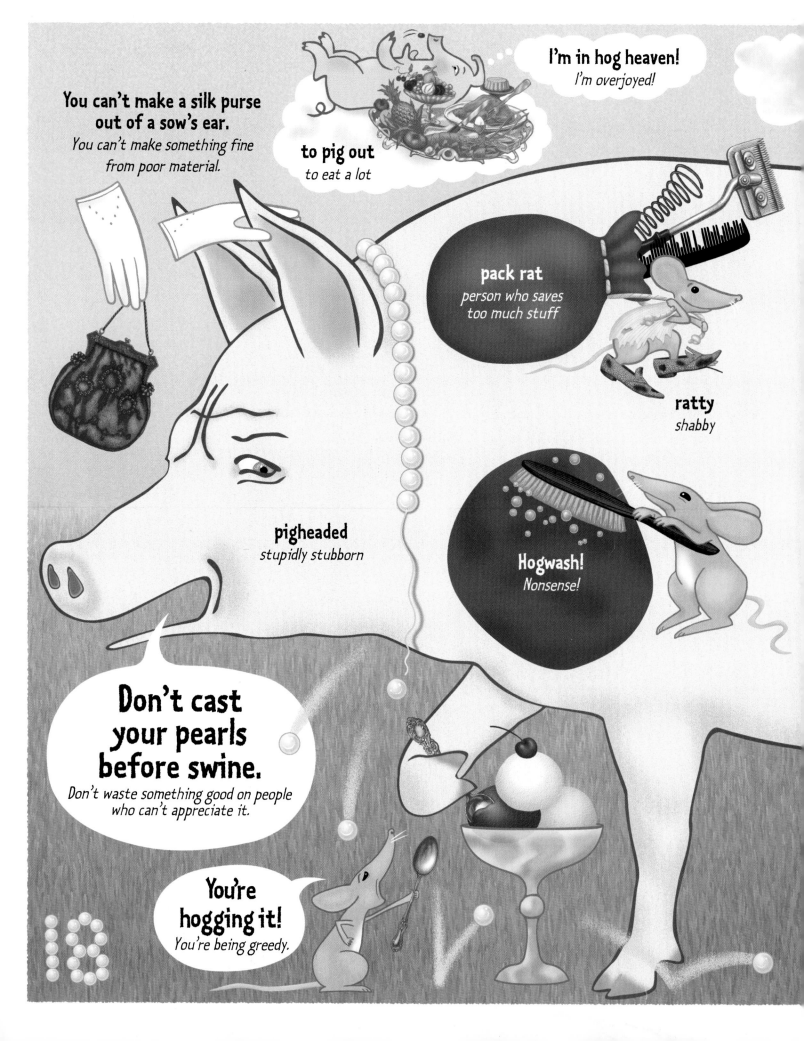

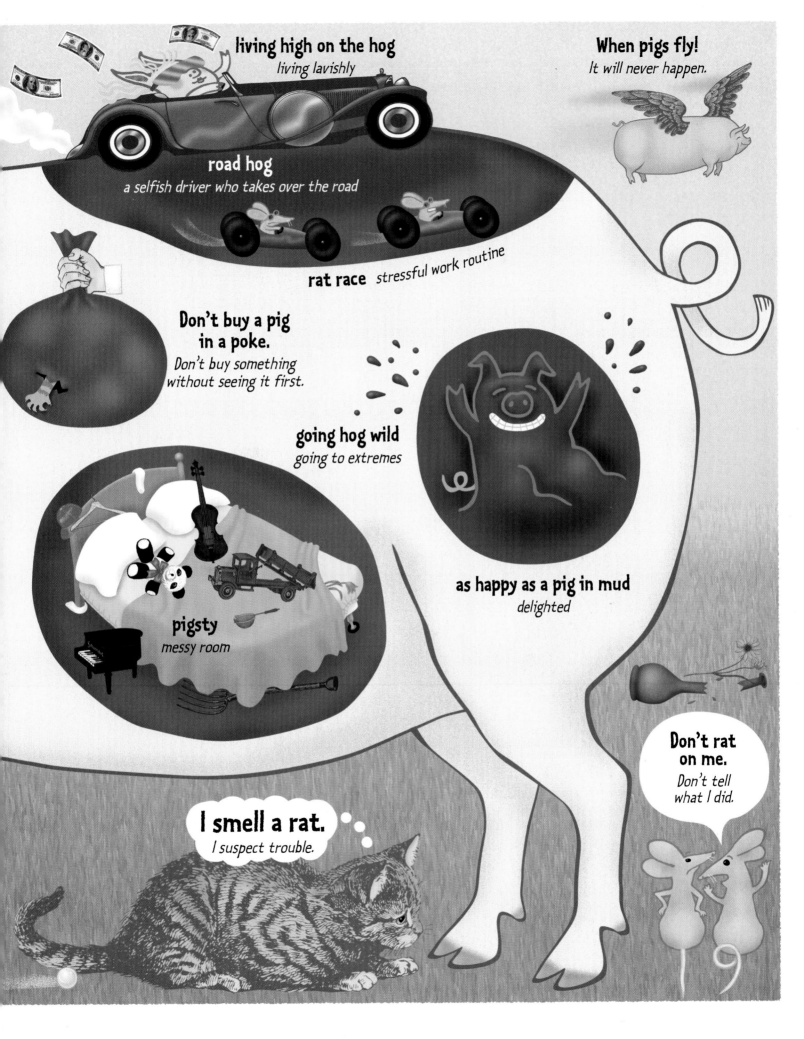

**one-horse town**
*tiny town*

**You're locking the barn door after the horse has been stolen.**
*You're taking precautions after it's too late.*

**horse sense**
*common sense*

**clotheshorse**
*well-dressed person*

**You're putting the cart before the horse.**
*You're doing things in the wrong order.*

**She's a one-trick pony.**
*She can do one thing well.*

**He's as stubborn as a mule.**
*He won't change his mind, no matter what.*

**Don't look a gift horse in the mouth.**
*Don't criticize a present you've received.*

**ponytail**
*hairstyle that looks like a pony's tail*

$20

He's a wolf in sheep's clothing.
*He's an enemy pretending to be a friend.*

as innocent as a lamb
*blameless*

**scapegoat**
*innocent person who gets blamed*

**She pulled the wool over his eyes.**
*She fooled him.*

**Separate the sheep from the goats.**
*Divide the good from the bad.*

**to butt heads**
*to argue fiercely*

**That will get his goat.**
*That will make him angry.*

**in two shakes of a lamb's tail**
*quickly*

**Butt out!**
*Mind your own business!*

**sheepish**
*embarrassed*

**to butt in**
*to intrude*

**to get fleeced**
*to be swindled*

23

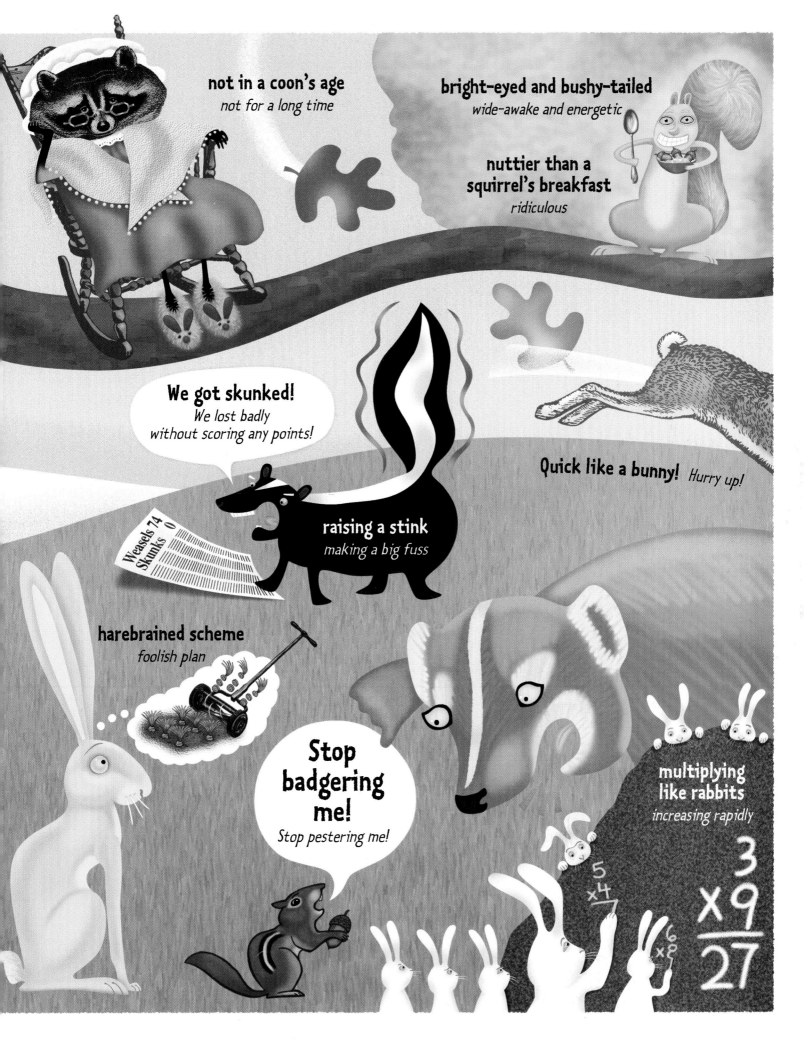

to cry wolf
*to give a false warning*

She runs like a deer.
*She is a fast runner.*

WOLF!

The buck stops here.
*I take full responsibility.*

as hungry as a bear
*very hungry*

He looked like a deer caught in the headlights.
*He was stunned.*

It's a bear.
*It's a difficult task.*

bear hug
*big hug*

She's not the average bear.
*She is unusual.*

**She fawns on him.**
*She slavishly tries to please him.*

**to lock horns**
*to disagree*

**He is crazy like a fox.**
*He seems foolish, yet he is outsmarting everyone.*

**as sly as a fox**
*clever*

**wolfing down food**
*eating too fast*

Unfair!

What are your demands?

**cub reporter**
*journalist who is new on the job*

**dumb bunny**
*stupid person*

**wildcat strike**
*unauthorized work stoppage*

**Put a tail on him.**
*Send a spy to follow him secretly.*

**eager beaver**
*enthusiastic person*

**to keep the wolf from the door**
*to provide food for one's family*

**busy beaver**
*hard worker*

**He's a lone wolf.**
*He likes to be alone.*

Grrrrr!

**She threw me to the wolves.**
*She abandoned me in a bad situation.*

29

**I've seen the elephant.**
*I've seen more than enough.*

**They have the herd instinct.**
*They follow the crowd.*

**When you hear hoofbeats, think horses, not zebras.**
*Try the simple solution first.*

**There's an elephant in the room.**
*There's a big problem nobody wants to face.*

**white elephant**
*fancy thing no one wants*

**Don't bury your head in the sand like an ostrich.**
*Don't hide from reality.*

**She has a memory like an elephant.**
*She won't forget.*

**The leopard can't change his spots.**
*A person's nature will stay the same.*

**zebra crossing**
*striped crosswalk*

**It's an 800-pound gorilla.**
*It's an uncontrollable problem.*

**It's more fun than a barrel of monkeys.**
*It's very enjoyable.*

**as brave as a lion**
*courageous*

Ha! Ha! Ha!

**to lionize someone**
*to treat someone like a celebrity*

**to laugh like a hyena**
*laughing loudly*

**the lion's share**
*the biggest portion*

**Don't let the camel get its nose under the tent.**
*Don't let something bad get started.*

**I have a tiger by the tail.**
*This problem is huge.*

**He is a paper tiger.**
*He seems strong, but he is actually weak.*

**grease monkey**
*mechanic*

**monkeyshines**
*mischievous tricks*

**to go ape**
*to act wildly*

**It threw a monkey wrench into our plans.**
*It ruined our plans.*

**They made a monkey out of me.**
*They made me look foolish.*

**monkey suit**
*tuxedo*

**monkey see, monkey do**
*to copy what other people do*

**kangaroo court**
*a court that ignores the law*

**It's a dinosaur.**
*It's out of date.*

**It's neither fish nor fowl.**
*It doesn't fit easily into any category.*

**fossil**
*old person or thing*

31

on the WING

**bird's-eye view**
*view from overhead*

**Keep an eagle eye on it.**
*Watch it carefully.*

**round-robin**
*project that's completed as different people add to it step-by-step*

# I'm as free as a bird.
*There's nothing I have to do right now.*

**It's as light as a feather.** *It weighs very little.*

**You could've knocked me down with a feather.**
*I was very surprised.*

**Birds of a feather flock together.**
*Similar people stick together.*

**I was sent on a wild-goose chase.**
I was asked to search for something that couldn't be found.

**Don't ruffle any feathers.**
Don't upset anyone.

**stool pigeon**
*police informer*

**just for a lark** *just for fun*

**as happy as a lark** *cheerful*

**to wing it**
*to improvise*

**crow's-feet**
*wrinkles in the corners of the eyes*

**I had to eat crow.**
*I had to admit I was wrong.*

**crow's nest**
*lookout platform*

**as the crow flies** *in a straight line*

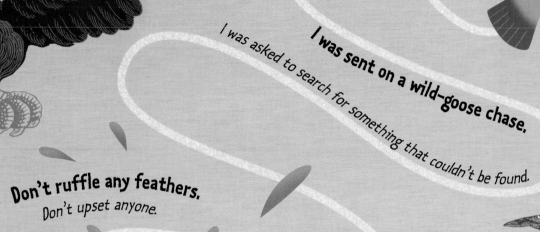

**to spread your wings**
*to become independent*

**to try your wings**
*to attempt a new skill*

**He's sitting in the catbird seat.**
*He has the advantage.*

**to feather your nest**
*to add to your wealth and comfort*

**I'm a lark.**
*I get up early in the morning.*

**We have an empty nest.**
*Our children have moved out.*

**as naked as a jaybird**
*not wearing any clothes*

**A bird in the hand is worth two in the bush.**
*Don't lose what you have by trying to get even more.*

**Watch it like a hawk.**
*Guard it carefully.*

**nest egg**
*savings for the future*

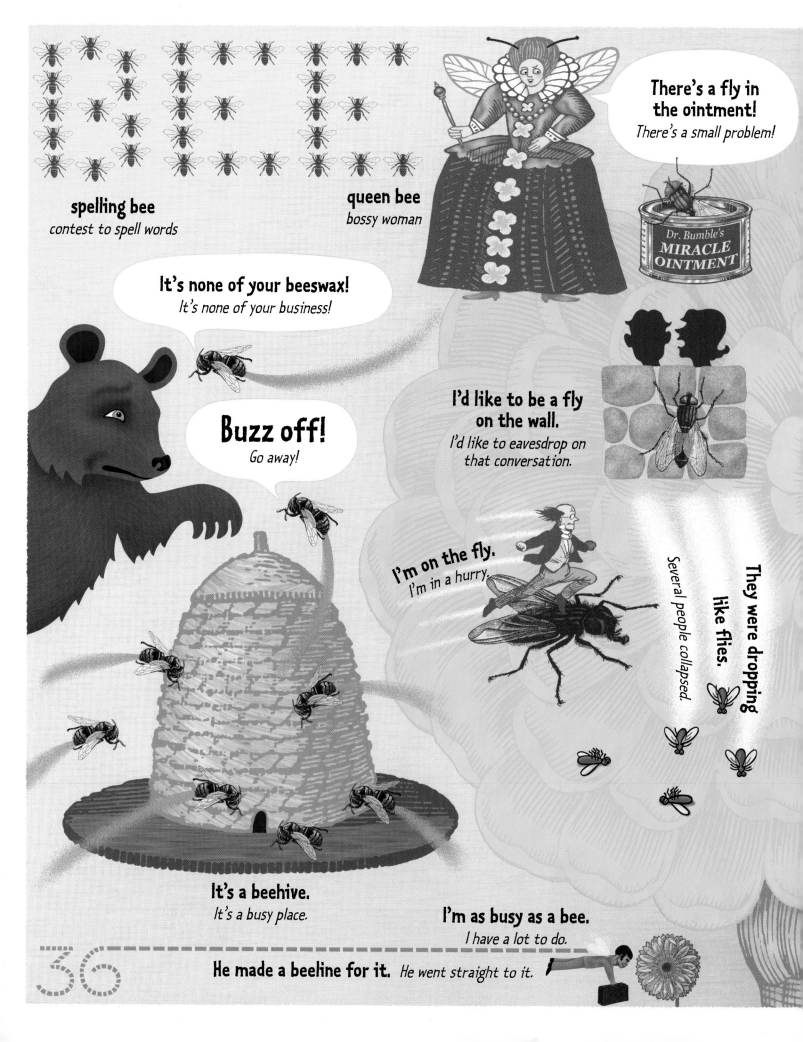

**She is a social butterfly.**
*She goes to lots of parties.*

**I have butterflies in my stomach.**
*I feel nervous.*

**as mad as a hornet**
*furious*

**You'll catch more flies with honey than with vinegar.**
*You'll get what you want by being nice, not by being mean.*

What's the Buzz? HONEY

BLUE LABEL VINEGAR
PRESERVERS ROCHESTER
CURTICE BROTHERS CO.
ROCHESTER, N.Y. USA

**to stir up a hornet's nest**
*to start a great deal of trouble*

**I was drawn like a moth to a flame.**
*I was fascinated.*

**moth-eaten**
*shabby*

**cocooning**
*retreating to the privacy of home*

down by the GROUND

**slugabed**
*someone who lingers in bed*

**sluggard**
*lazy person*

**sluggish**
*slow moving*

**You're opening a can of worms!**
*You're bringing up a problem that will lead to more problems!*

**snail mail**
*postal delivery*

**at a snail's pace**
*very slowly*

World's Best WORMS

**worm's-eye view**
*view from a low point*

Now I know!

**The early bird catches the worm.**
*Start before others do for the best chance of success.*

**He wormed it out of me.**
*He persuaded me to tell.*

**That was when you were knee-high to a grasshopper.**
*That was when you were a small child.*

**antsy**
*restless*

**toad-strangler**
*heavy rainfall*

**He has ants in his pants.**
*He is fidgeting.*

**If it was a snake, it would have bitten you.**
*The item you were searching for is right there—you just didn't see it.*

you look wonderful.....What is your secret?

**She's a toady.**
*She flatters powerful people to gain favor.*

**snake in the grass**
*hidden enemy*

This cures baldness, bad breath, itchy fur.....

**snake oil**
*product that doesn't work as advertised*

**He speaks with a forked tongue.**
*He is lying.*

**mole**
*spy*

Kure ALL
PREVENTS SNAKE BITES

It's too high to climb!

**He is lower than a snake's belly.**
*He is dishonest.*

**Don't make a mountain out of a molehill.**
*Don't exaggerate a problem.*

Digging It 39
Composting Fun
Cooking with Dirt

**bookworm**
*someone who loves to read*

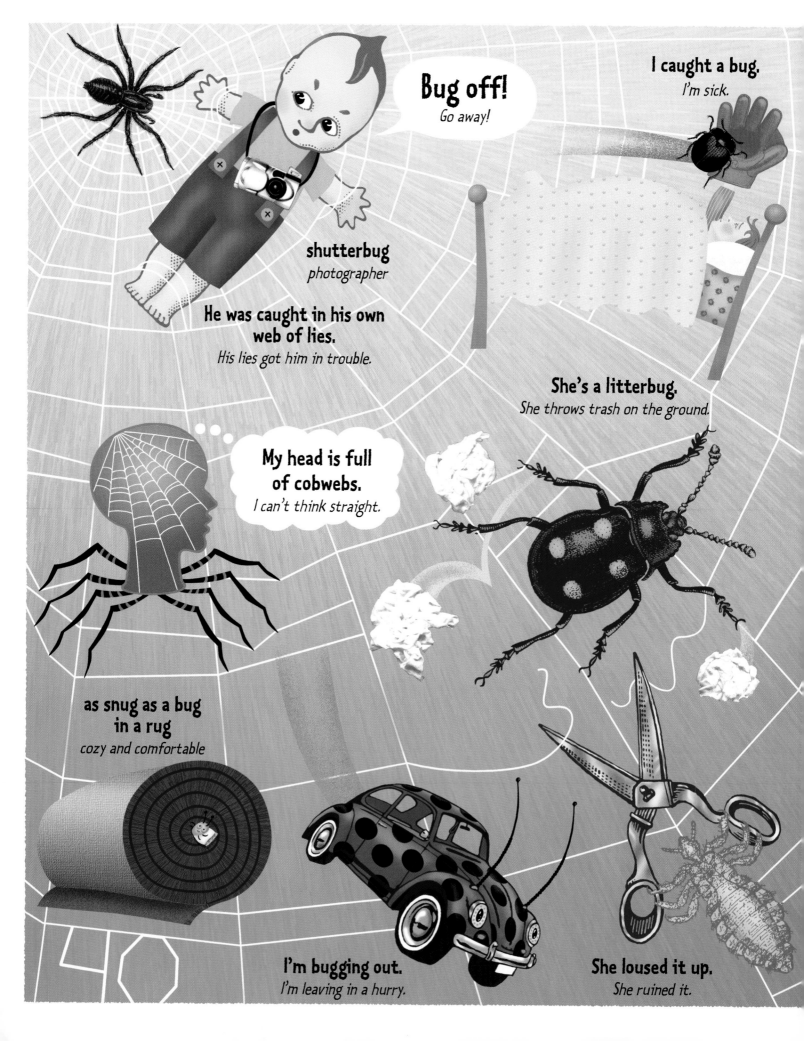

**After a while, crocodile!**
*Good-bye to you, too!*

**They were like rats leaving a sinking ship.**
*They left in a hurry.*

**If you swim with the sharks, you'll get bitten.**
*If you spend time with bad people, you'll get hurt.*

**water rat**
*good swimmer*

**I have other fish to fry.**
*I have better things to do.*

**cold fish**
*unemotional person*

**He's on a fishing expedition.**
*He's trying to get information.*

**It's a red herring.**
*It's an attempt to distract us from the real issue.*

**You look green around the gills.**
*You look ill.*

**He's not the only fish in the sea.**
*He's not the only possibility.*

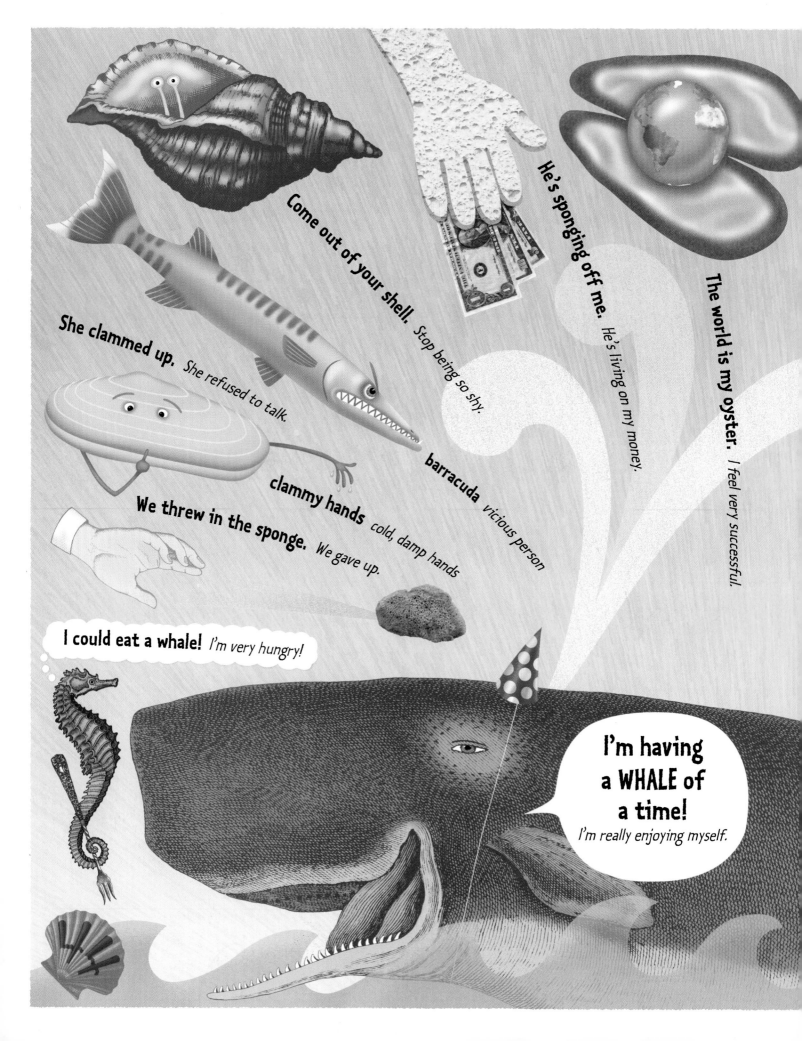

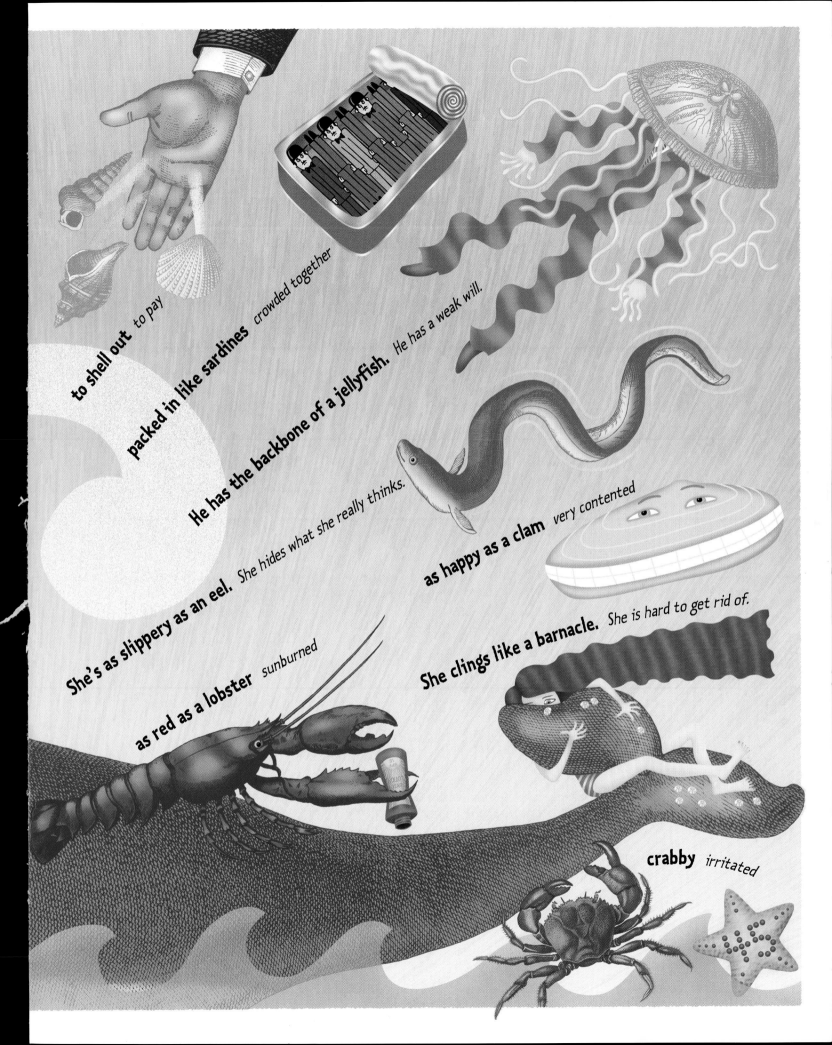

to shell out  *to pay*

packed in like sardines  *crowded together*

He has the backbone of a jellyfish.  *He has a weak will.*

She's as slippery as an eel.  *She hides what she really thinks.*

as happy as a clam  *very contented*

as red as a lobster  *sunburned*

She clings like a barnacle.  *She is hard to get rid of.*

crabby  *irritated*

**If wishes were horses,
then beggars would ride.**
*Desire alone won't make dreams happen.*

**pet project**
*favorite project*

My crayon broke again!

**pet peeve**
*repeated complaint*

**teacher's pet**
*favored student*

**the black sheep
of the family**
*the worst member of the family*

WANTED

**catcalls**
*loud yells of disapproval*

Boo!
Boo!
Boo!

**She wouldn't hurt a fly.**
*She is gentle.*

**The best-laid plans of mice and men oft go astray.**
*Even careful plans can go wrong.*

**I'll be a monkey's uncle!**
*I'm amazed!*

**It's driving me batty.**
*I'm frustrated with it.*

**I'm as blind as a bat.**
*My vision is poor.*

**donkey work**
*hard physical labor*

For my feline friends—
Esme, Deli, Abby, Cleo, and Photon
L. L.
And for mine—
Skeezix and Dunkelman
P. S.

Text copyright © 2003 by Loreen Leedy and Pat Street

Illustrations copyright © 2003 by Loreen Leedy

All Rights Reserved

Printed in the United States of America

www.holidayhouse.com

First Edition

Library of Congress Cataloging-in-Publication Data

Leedy, Loreen.

There's a frog in my throat: 440 animal sayings a little bird told me

by Loreen Leedy and Pat Street; illustrated by Loreen Leedy.—1st ed.

p. cm.

Includes index.

ISBN: 0-8234-1774-3

1. English language—Terms and phrases—Juvenile literature.

2. Zoology—Nomenclature (Popular)—Juvenile literature.

3. Animals—Folklore—Juvenile literature.

4. Figures of speech—Juvenile literature. [1. English language—Terms and phrases.

2. Figures of speech. 3. Animals—Folklore.]

I. Street, Pat. II. Title.

PE1583.L39 2003

428.1-dc21    2002068920

**I'm bullish.**
*I think stock market prices will go up.*

**I'm bearish.**
*I think stock market prices will go down.*

48

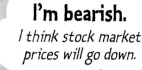

**the tail end**
*the very end*